MW01595417

MY NAME IS NOAH
Stories Before the Flood
Volume III

By
James L. Eakins
Ozark, Missouri

My Name is Noah

Stories Before the Flood
Volume III

Copyright © 2024 by James L. Eakins
ISBN 979-8-9920492-6-8
First Printing 2025

A novella - a realistic fiction story

Published by:
James L. Eakins
Ozark, Mo 65721

Printed in the United States of America

Irwin Printing Company
260 NE US Highway 60
Billings, Missouri 65610

DEDICATION

To my Lord and Savior, Jesus Christ, I dedicate this book, who tells us, "As it was in the days of Noah, so shall it be also in the days of the Son of man."

They ate, drank, and married wives; they were given in marriage until the day Noah entered the ark, and the flood came and destroyed them all.

J.E.

ACKNOWLEDGMENTS

I am deeply thankful to the Holy Spirit for guiding and inspiring me to continue writing.

With love and appreciation:

-James

ABOUT THE AUTHOR

James L. Eakins was born on December 4, 1953, to Guy and Martha Jane Eakins in the small town of Ozark, Missouri, where he spent his childhood and attended school. In 1975, he married Judy Johnson from Galena,Missouri, and they eventually became the proud parents of seven beautiful children: Galen, Misty, Rachel, Benjamin, Joshua, Charity, and Judy Kaylee.

He gave his life to Christ in 1978 and was quickly inspired to lead souls to Jesus. He began a personal ministry of soul-winning, going door-to-door to share the gospel and distribute tracts. Responding to God's call to preach, he held his first revival later that year, marking the start of his evangelistic travels within a 250-mile radius of his home, preaching in any church where God opened the door.

James began his pastoral journey at McCord Bend Southern Baptist Mission Church. He was then led to Wheelerville Union Church, which quickly grew to the point of overflowing. An old-fashioned Brush Arbor was built at Scholten Corner, not far away, to accommodate the growing congregation. Night after night, the Spirit of God moved powerfully, igniting a revival that swept through the countryside and transformed countless lives for eternity. Ultimately, God guided him to purchase a storefront building on Main Street in Crane, Missouri, where he founded New Life Fellowship Church in 1985.

As cassette tapes gained popularity, God provided him with a way to record and replicate his sermons for widespread distribution. He began offering these free sermon tapes at his church, during his revivals, door-to-door, and by mail upon request. This outreach generated numerous phone calls inviting him to preach in various locations. In 1987, Touching the World Ministries was established, marking the start of a new era of travel and adventure. He preached in many churches across the United States, including several Native American Indian Reservation churches. His ministry also took him to Central America, where he led a significant crusade in Belize City and held revivals in Dangriga and the surrounding areas, transforming the lives of countless individuals.

Feeling called by God to provide more consistent and in-depth ministry to the Native American community, rather than making occasional visits, he moved his family to Pyramid Lake in Nixon, Nevada, in 1990, where he ministered to and served the Paiute Indians on the reservation.

He later spent three years pastoring the Calvary Assembly of God Church in Gardnerville, Nevada, situated in the Carson Valley. During this period, he launched a new initiative to spread the gospel through printed materials. The church created and published a multi-page newspaper and distributed it for free.

In 1994, he returned to his hometown and founded the Ozark Full Gospel Church, where he continues to serve as pastor to this day. Since then, he has launched numerous initiatives, including a Christian school, five revival outreach centers, several radio broadcasts, and the Ozarks' Good News newspaper. His sermons air on television every Sunday morning and are available on CDs, DVDs, podcasts, and live streams, as well as on Facebook and YouTube. He is an avid reader and a diligent Bible student, making him a self-taught and self-inflicted scholar of the Bible. He is widely recognized for his in-depth Bible teaching and preaching; hundreds of thousands of his messages are still distributed worldwide.

James is the author of numerous newspaper articles and sermon booklets, as well as the books "Run Chicken Run," "Brush with Glory," "Unique Stories from My Ozark Childhood," "My Name is Adam," "My Name is Methuselah," "Visitors From Another Dimension," and "Simple Poems of Life."

Don't proofread my life
unless it is for a
glorious publication.

~ James L. Eakins

PREFACE

The Bible's creation story is true; however, my stories include a lot of fiction. "My Name is Noah" is based on the actual Biblical tale of Noah before the flood. I've taken great care not to contradict the clear truths recorded in the Bible.

Remember, this isn't a Bible commentary; it shares the beautiful story of humanity before the flood as if Noah were telling his personal story. My deepest wish is to inspire your mind to think bigger and explore more possibilities.

These stories will answer many of your questions and deepen your understanding of humanity's origins. My goal is to inspire you and renew your perspective on God's past interactions with people. So, keep reading, enjoy, and may God's blessings flood your heart.

J.E.

In the beginning,

God created the heavens and the earth.

Therefore, I have no trouble

believing the rest of the Bible.

~ James L. Eakins

MY NAME IS NOAH
Stories Before the Flood

Volume III

A great flood is coming.

The waters of the heavens

will meet the waters of earth.

We build a vessel to survive the storm.

We build an ark.

~ Noah

Stories Before the Flood
My Name Is Noah

Wow, my wildest dreams are coming true, and boy, am I scared and confused. A great flood is approaching. The waters of the heavens will clash with the waters of the earth. I will build a ship to survive the storm, as God has commanded me to do the unsinkable. He has ordered me to construct a massive ship, which he calls an ark, and then fill it with every kind of land animal on Earth, because he is going to destroy the Earth with a worldwide flood. I've always known and dreamed, since childhood, that God had an important task for me to fulfill, but I never in a million years expected this. I did not realize that my love for animals and my ability to build large things with wood were preparing me for God's saving grace, as He destroys this corrupt world.

As God speaks to me, I am both terrified and sickened in the pit of my stomach. But in my grief and fear comes an extraordinary excitement. It will take years to build an ark of this magnitude, and to get it to hold together in raging, hostile waters and keep it afloat with so much cargo will be nothing short of a miracle.

Truly, God has called on me to build the unsinkable ship.

When I told my father, Lamech, and my grand-father, Methuselah, that the ship would be 300 cubits long, 50 cubits wide, and 30 cubits high, they were shocked and overwhelmed. Then I informed them that God had instructed me to include one pair of every kind of unclean animal and seven pairs of every kind of clean animal in the ark, along with large stores of food. My father said, "This thing that God calls an ark is big enough to house two whole villages." (520 feet long, 85 feet wide, and 51 feet high). "This will cost a fortune to build." Then my father promised to cover all of the expenses and even provide workers to assist with the labor. Wow, it was already coming together. My father owned cattle, vineyards, and orchards on a thousand hills. Still, this command from God will require a great deal of study, hard work, sweat, and seeking God's will through many prayers.

Grandfather Methuselah In Tears

When my grandfather Methuselah heard this, he began to cry and said to me through tears, "I have preached with my father Enoch and with you. This is a great honor for all of us, and I will help you with the Master's plan, all drafts, measurements, and diagrams. It will take years of planning as God gives his instructions." My grandfather, Methuselah, was brilliant and skilled in many things, including engineering and building. He told me that the preparations for this ship are critical.

Later, I found this to be true; it took just over two decades to make the diagrams, floor plans, ground plans, and drafts to determine the amount and size of gopher wood for this giant three-story ark.

Coating the entire ship, both inside and out, with pitch to make it waterproof would be a significant challenge. Finding sticky, waterproof materials like pitch and tree resin would be a major task for Lamech's everyday workers. My three little boys had a fantastic time playing in this sticky pitch, and when they got it in their hair, their mother was not amused.

When the three boys were born, I was 500 years old, and their mother and I were shocked when they came into our lives as triplets. Japheth looked nothing like Shem and Ham, but Shem and Ham looked identical. Ham was the last to be born. These boys will grow up under the shadow of the Great Ark. It was here that they learned to play, work, and live for God. I have no idea who invented this rare game of hide and seek, but they would play it for hours in the safety of the ark. One day, Ham hid in one of the large semi-empty pitch barrows. Oh, my, he smelled wonderful from the tree resin, but he was sticky for days, with everything sticking to him, even the gnats and flies, and it wouldn't wash off. Once again, their mother was quite irate with the boys, especially Ham, who was covered from head to toe.

God remembered me,

my family,

and our animals.

~ Noah
(Ref: Genesis 8:1)

You can only hold your breath so long,

under the dark waters of sin.

You will drown in deep regret

if you don't surface to God's demands.

~ James L. Eakins

Years At The Drafting Table

While Methuselah, my grandfather, sat with me at my large drafting table, we rehearsed God's commands concerning this ship. It was to be 300 cubits long, 50 cubits wide, and 30 cubits high, with three stories. One cubit is the length from my elbow to my middle finger. I am a huge man, so my cubit would be much larger than that of some average-sized men. My grandfather stressed to me the importance of building the ark correctly the first time. "You have only one chance," he said, "It must hold up against the wind and raging waters, and float above the devastating waters; it must be unsinkable." There was to be only one door on the side, large enough to reach as high as the top of the first floor. There would be small one-cubit windows all around the top of the ark for ventilation and light. I did mention to Methuselah that I would need one window at the very top of the ark to look up to God in hope and prayer. It would be helpful for this personal window to be connected to a special covering that could be dismantled when we arrive on land again in the New World.

We worked for years on these drafts and diagrams; each measurement was carefully calculated and finely tuned. We needed to consider cages for each kind of animal, as well as food and water storage. Lighting was also a major concern, and finding a way to intake acceptable fresh water while expelling animal waste outside of the ark was the most significant challenge.

The giants and the men of renown came to confront us again and offer their expertise. They said, "They wanted to help us save the world, for we have a better way." These fallen angels and giants were desperately trying to save their offspring from being destroyed. This time it was not me, but my father, Lamech, who chased them off, and boy, was he furious and abrasive with them; he hated the giants, and later on, he would blame them for his wife's horrific murder.

Early Timber To Season

While we prepared for the ark's construction, many of Lamech's workers had already begun cutting and delivering timber to two slightly sloped hillsides. These hillsides conveniently overlooked the designated building and launch site for the ark. Often, I had to stop what I was doing and warn my three boys not to play around the large pile of tree logs, lest they get hurt. We continued to slowly work out the details before actual construction began. It took just over twenty years to complete the detailed construction drawings, which included all the precise measurements and necessary materials. My three sons were born just seven years before our plans for the ark were finally completed. Ham was filled with wonder over these diagrams and drawings of the ark. He was at the "why?" stage. His mother and I told him that God was going to destroy the world with a great flood. He asked, "Why?" and we explained why. He cried and asked, "What about us?" We told him that God had commanded us to build a ship and that he would save our favorite animals and our family. He replied, "Oh, ok," and then went outside to play with his brothers.

Finally, our construction plans for the building were complete. The building of the ark was now in full swing.

Constructing the ship's frame along with the inner and outer walls didn't take long. From the beginning, we applied pitch both inside and outside every joint and all overlapping wood. My boys, for the most part, just wanted to play and often got in the way. As the boys grew older, they began to work and developed excellent skills in many areas.

When I first started building the ark, I got blisters all over my hands, at least until they became calloused. Then there were the awful splinters that my wife had to dig out of my fingers every night with her sharp knife, along with the boys' splinters, too.

One late evening, I was fitting a large, heavy beam into one of the load-bearing walls when it slipped and nearly crushed my thumb off. The pain was so intense that it made me feel sick. Not knowing what to do, I dipped my smashed thumb into a barrel of sticky pitch, wrapped a rag around it, and went home. My wife was beside herself and was not pleased that I had dipped my injured thumb in pitch. She insisted on cleaning all that pitch off and out of my nasty wound, warning me that it needed to be cleaned up before an infection set in. As Emzara started scrubbing my thumb vigorously, I insisted on a strong drink, but my request was denied. She said sarcastically, "Oh, boohoo- don't be a crybaby, you are not dying." Once she got my smashed thumb cleaned up from the sweaty blood and dirty pitch, she dipped my thumb in pure lemon juice and sprinkled salt on it. The pain reminded me of the three-foot scorpion that had bitten and stung me at the lumberyard while I was sorting boards. God eventually healed my thumb, but not without a lot of pain and suffering.

The interior construction of the ark progressed much more slowly. It has three stories, necessitating three floors strong enough to support tons of weight. We spent years installing a freshwater system and devising a method to remove unwanted waste, which presented a significant challenge. My sons took on the task of building feed bends and large cages for each type of animal. Pitch was continually applied to the ship's hull inside and outside; it had to be sealed and watertight.

Methuselah reminded me that this ship is so gigantic that it will require all the animals to be distributed evenly by their weight. Drogue stones should hang outside the ship on both sides to sift the water currents, and a large bow fin should be placed on top at the rear. This large fin will guide the ship into the wind. A stern fin must also be added on the opposite end, submerged underwater, along with three deep keels that must run the full length of the vessel, positioned on the very belly of the ship. All this will prevent the ark from rolling over, thank God! I followed all of Methuselah's instructions.

Noah's Ark

was our chance

to one day live

and meet our Savior

~ James Eakins

My Sons Find Their Wives

The actual construction of the ark has now been a long, hard 80 years, and it's time for Shem, Ham, and Japheth to find a God-fearing wife. It has always been my custom to have no work on the 7th day of the week. These days off each week would be an excellent time for my sons to seek out a wife. We have built four large living quarters inside the ark, one for my wife, Emzara, and me, and one each for my sons with their wives. But here are the rules for seeking a wife. The woman must fear God and come to see the ark in its construction, then listen to my mandate, which I have received from the Lord. If she believes and the woman has God's approval, **"That is if she doesn't frantically run away."** Then my son can take her and make her his wife.

Japheth was the first to find a godly wife, and this girl knew in her heart that God was about to destroy the face of the entire Earth. The first time she looked at the ark, she cried and thanked God for a chance to live and serve Him. My wife and Rayneh became the best of friends.

Finding a wife took Shem much longer; his pick-up line for the girls was a bit frightening. I later learned he was telling the ladies, "Come with me or you're going to die." You must admit that this statement was true, but it had to be a strange turn-off. The first woman that Shem convinced to visit the ark and hear my mandate ran away like a jackrabbit over the hillside, screaming and yelling that we were all crazy and delusional. It was the next lady that Shem brought home to see us and the ark whom he wed. Her name is Aryel, and she is lovely and godly. She believed God's warning and was thankful to become a part of God's plan for a new world.

But poor, poor Ham had immense difficulties finding a wife. He brought no fewer than ten women to see the ark project, and all of them were either crazy or godless or both. Most of these women attempted to escape as quickly as possible. I later learned that Ham was visiting the giants and heard about their plans to build a Great Pyramid, which they never executed. However, Ham had told me that the giants were constructing something massive deep beneath the Earth's surface. Ham was so intrigued by the pyramid's construction drawings that he managed to sneak a copy of these detailed plans onto the ark. After many heartbreaks, Ham finally found a godly woman. Her name is Kezia. She is cute, ambitious, and enthusiastic, and she immediately helped finish up the living quarters for her and Ham on the ark. My wife, Emzara, assisted all three girls in preparing their temporary homes in the ark.

During this time, God had temporarily suspended the fertilization of all the ark's females until after the flood, and only then could they bring forth children, except for the stowaway rats and mice. God had other plans for them.

The friends and relatives of Shem's, Ham's, and Japheth's wives were constantly coming around the ship, mocking and trying to get the girls to abandon their husbands, declaring that all of us are insane. Kezia's father would come around drunk and demand that his daughter return home with him. However, Kezia remained convinced of God's imminent coming wrath. Her father came so frequently that Ham finally had to forcibly remove Kezia's father from the ship's building site. It was a very nasty and angry encounter. I felt very sorry for Kezia's father, knowing that as a little boy, his twin sister and two of his little brothers were burned to death by some of the giant's offspring. I'm sure that drunkenness was his way of coping with the pain of his past. This world has become a very violent and wicked place for all mankind.

We worked hard to construct special rooms in the ark, including a kitchen for preparing food, various storage spaces for unique seeds, and areas for growing easy-to-cultivate vegetables. We also took along a box containing a small swarm of honeybees and fed them some of our honey during the journey. Additionally, we built a tool shop and a blacksmith workshop, a library for all documents, paintings, and scrolls, and a storage room to preserve the writings of Enoch, Adam, Seth, Jared, Methuselah, and others.

Puritan John Owen
tearfully admonished his people,
"Get you an ark.

Prepare an ark for you
and your family's safety.

The ark is Jesus Christ.

There is no other way.

There Will Be No Wine On Board The Ark

My father, Lamech, taught me how to grow fruit trees and grape vineyards and make wine as a young boy. Being a little too often given to wine, I forbid myself from drinking wine while preparing the ark. It was a strict rule that none of our workers in and around the ark were permitted to drink wine. There was to be a standing rule that no wine was to be stored around or on board the ark.

All three of my sons worked hard every day building on the ark while their great-grandfather, Methuselah, watched and helped when he could. My boys had one day off a week and made the best of it. They decided from time to time to go into the city and pretend to preach a little bit. They were always getting into fights with the giants and the ungodly people. When the men of the city would start mocking me and their grandfathers, my sons would bust heads. When people would laugh and call the building of the ark a ridiculous ship, my sons would bust heads; they were not good with words, but they could bust heads. Working long, hard days on the ark made Shem, Ham, and Japheth very strong and muscled up.

Ham was big and hot-headed, easily stirred to fight. All three of my sons were strong and large men, and Ham, being the biggest, could hold his own against the Nephilim. Shem and Japheth, however, seemed to receive additional help from the Lord. With the boys drinking wine and fighting, their mother and I often found ourselves stirred to pray. Their great-grand-father Methuselah said, "Not to worry, when these boys get shut up in the ark and the flood comes, these great-grandsons of mine will learn humility and patience as they feed and clean up after the animal deposits, and of course, the women folk will help tame them too."

My Father Lamech Dies

I received word during the night that my father, Lamech, had passed away suddenly and without warning. My sons were devastated and completely shocked; their grandfather was only 777 years old.

My mother and grandmother were very godly women; however, they had both passed away. Methuselah's wife (my grandmother) died many years before the boys were born. My mother was murdered while Shem, Ham, and Japheth were still infants. Lamech, my father, never discovered who had brutally taken her life. But he always blamed the giants.

The boys were deeply concerned about their great-grandfather Methuselah, who was now 964 years old and whose health was declining rapidly. Because of Enoch's prophecy regarding the naming of Methuselah, I knew we were running out of time.

Since I was my father's firstborn, all of Lamech's property, orchards, and vineyards were now mine. Thus, I quickly summoned all of the workers in my father's vineyards and beyond to report to the ark's site for the finishing touches. I needed them to apply a double coat of pitch both on the outside and inside of the ark's shell. Strong ramps needed to be built with a gradual incline leading up to the ark's massive door. This ramp must also be extensive, allowing animals of every kind to enter the ark.

There can be no mistakes, and I still haven't figured out how to collect all the animals. But I now see an unusual number of animals in our forest and open fields. The sky is filled with all kinds of birds. We have to shoo or herd some of these animals away from the ark just to be able to finish the work on the ark. God wants one pair, of male and female, of every unclean kind. Seven pairs of every kind of clean animal. He also wants the foul of the air included, and how I shut the great massive door of the ark when we are loaded is beyond me. I'm very nervous, now that the time is running out, my father's workers will be of extreme importance at this late hour. When preaching to the workers, they laughed and made light of my warnings. Even my siblings and my wife's siblings laugh at me and mock me. All the workers just wanted to work for money, so they could eat, drink, and be merry. They all thought I was crazy and out of my mind. These will be the nearest people to me who will beg, scream, and cry to get in the ark after the door is closed. But they will all die under the flooding wrath of God.

The Wind Was Blowing, And The Animals Were Starting To Press In

It was pretty apparent that the animals were beginning to gather all around the ark. Every kind of animal was already inhabiting our landmass due to the greenhouse effect, thriving in a perfect environment for each species. Around us, there were many great forests and dense vegetation as well. Simply put, these animals were scattered not just all over the world but also in our homeland.

My wife and my son's wives were already gathering the small, helpless, cute, and cuddly animals into the ark, placing them into their smaller cages, and there were numerous smaller animals; this helped speed up the loading process. During that week, the larger animals began to enter the ark of safety. Ham's wife, Kezia, the feisty one, was proactive in gathering the lizards, reptiles, and similar animals, which expedited the loading process. All the cages and bins were ready to be filled. Hay and grain had been stored. Methuselah had prepared tons of exceptional non-meat food that the meat-eating animals would enjoy. Shem's wife, Aryel, found butterflies, hummingbirds, and other unique little animals, all to accelerate the main week of entrance into the ark. Some of the small cages for the reptiles included breeding boxes for insects, such as mealworms and crickets, to nurture and feed them.

There will be no little guy left behind, not even a land snail or a slow turtle; all of us are preparing for the big day. Spiders, bees, and ants, bumblebees, and similar insects, "without an invitation," had already made their home in the rafters of the ark. We fed the bumblebees some of our honey along the way.

Methuselah watches in wonder as the busy gathering of small animals unfolds, noticing how the girls pursue the smaller and more helpless creatures living around the home place.

My grandfather Methuselah said to me," Noah, my son, God will bring the animals to the ark that he wants saved and their kind." Then he said to me, "Son, I will not be going with you." A few days later, the animals began to come into the ark by the thousands. I'm sure unseen angels were working all around us. The ramps were done, the food was stored, and everything was ready. Shem and his wife, Japheth and his wife, Ham and his wife, and my wife and I were working furiously to keep order in the ark as the small and great animals came into the ark to be saved.

Every creature was made docile, for God had them in complete control. The giant animals were mainly unclean. God only required one pair of them, consisting of a male and a female. We noticed that the bigger breeds were just weaned and not fully grown. Some of these animals will grow much bigger than the elephant, and I don't know how they will survive in a new world that is initially short of animals and heavy vegetation. Even the giraffes had shorter necks, as if they had been prepared for such a time as this. Methuselah was delighted and could hardly contain his composure as he watched God fill the ark.

Remember,

temptation to sin is a nasty scam.

~ James Eakins

Grandfather Methuselah Dies, And The Rain Begins

Days later, my grandfather Methuselah died while I was waiting inside the ark. In my grief, a beautiful white dove rested on my right shoulder. Up above in the rafters, I heard a "rain crow," "ka, ka, ka, ka, kow, kow, kowlp, kowlp!" Then the rain started, and God slammed the massive door shut. Methuselah was 969 years old, and I am now 600 years old.

It's storming and raining hard, the Earth is shaking, and I hear loud, constant booming thunder. The exploding lightning and thunder are so intense and loud that I can feel them vibrating in my chest. I couldn't even hear myself think, and we were terrified. I'm sure God has put some animals in hibernation for their safety. The rushing water, lightning, and thunder were sickening and terrifying. I'm praying this ship holds together.

Helpless people are screaming, crying, and even cursing on the outside, begging me to let them in, but God had shut the door, and it's too late for them; they are now stranded on the outside to suffer God's wrath. We will be in shock and awe for many days, especially the first forty days and forty nights. These horrific cries of fear, the screaming and begging to get inside the ark, will haunt us in our hearts for the rest of our lives.

God had given them fair warning through Enoch, Methuselah, and many others. He had given them well over a hundred and twenty years to repent and look to him.

But they had no time for God and His Holiness. They loved their sins and pleasures, loving to eat, drink, and be merry. **Temptation to sin is a nasty scam!**

The Earth shook violently, and the ark vibrated inside and out, while the lightning and thunder constantly roared. We were in the dark for weeks, our lamps were a great blessing, and the constant lightning helped, too. We did have some artificial lighting invented by renowned men, but soon it would lose its power and become nothing but disposable trash. Methuselah devised some temporary lighting, but it will also be diminished in this flood. But we still will have our lamps of fire, and God will grant us some supernatural light from time to time. Our eyes will also adjust to many of the dimly lit places. After all, we still maintain some of our incredible health, which was given to us in the days of Adam. We stayed busy to keep our minds off the raging waters outside. The ark never leaked, but during the first forty days, it required extensive repairs and cleanup inside. It was a brutal ride.

A Lot Of Water
But No Fish To Eat

After about the third day in the storm, we started to get hungry. What's ironic is that we had all this water and no fish to eat. We couldn't even see outside, let alone go fishing. However, God has allowed us to eat all the eggs we want, but we could never bring ourselves to eat some of the eggs, if you know what I mean.

It was understood from the beginning that there was to be no wine on board the ark; water was just fine. We found that potatoes, green beans, and other greens were easy to grow on the third floor. We had wheat, barley, and corn to make bread, and some of the animals' food could be shared with us. On rare occasions, we would eat one of the small clean animals, but we were cautious not to endanger a species. When we kill and eat a small animal, it saddens our day. On a brighter note, the womenfolk were outstanding at preparing our meals. In time, we developed a peaceful routine: working, praying, singing, resting, playing, eating, and returning to work.

The work on board the ark was hard; feeding and

caring for the animals was stressful and complicated. Removing all the animal waste was stinky, messy, and disgusting, but it had to be done. However, don't think our time on the ark was all bad; we had fun working and playing together. My sons were now 100 years old, but they played like children at times. Sometimes they would play an old game they used to play on this same ark, "Hide and Seek," only they didn't count up to just 10 with their eyes closed anymore, it was more like counting up to 50, then shouting, "Ready or not, here I come." All three boys would play this same game with their wives as well. The girls loved to play this game. Shem and his wife would go on pretend dates to the far end of the ark, sometimes the top floor, sometimes the lower floors. Ham's wife, Kezia, was always saying, "We are on a wonderful adventure." Many of the animals had become playful and became our pets. The grumpy animals had their sweet side too, and the birds were delightful to watch, but not to clean up after. Some of the pets we let roam the ark during the day, as long as they returned to their cages at bedtime. Of course, each night they had to be accounted for. My wife, Emzara, assigned daily duties to each of the three girls among the small animals. Kezia was always carrying around one of these cute little critters.

"Noah was so shut in
that no evil could reach him.
Floods did but lift him heavenward,
and winds did but waft him on his way."

~ Charles H. Spurgeon
(1834-1892)

By perseverance,
the snail reached the Ark.

~ Charles Spurgeon
(1834-1892)

Flowers And Music
On Board The Ark

Aryel and Rayneh created a flower bed using some of the rich dirt we had previously loaded on board, to which they added a sprinkle of seeds from our seed room. The women were delighted when the seeds sprouted. The flowers they produced were beautiful. However, they were later saddened when tiny stowaway bugs emerged from the soil and began to eat the flowers. We were then made aware of more stowaway bugs on our animals. Wouldn't you know it! There are just some things you cannot escape. Insects and worms were not collected and housed on the Ark. They do not have nostrils to breathe air and can survive the flood underground or on floating debris, such as dead carcasses. No doubt many of these insects hopped on board with us anyway. So, that reduced the number of species. Our ark became filled with stowaway rats and mice; they became treats for our meat-eating animals.

The first forty days and nights were awful, but the rain, wind, thunder, and lightning finally stopped. However, the Earth still shook, and the raging flood waters kept crashing and rushing upon the mountains for the next 150 days and nights; it has now been a total of 110 days and nights. After all this, it will be much smoother sailing. Cleanups and repairs will be less needed and much easier. Still no leaks, just spills and bad deals, inside. But, hey, Kezia keeps reminding us, "We are on a wonderful and exciting adventure." However, many days of feeling lonely and abandoned will disturb us. It's a good thing we have each other and our pet animal friends. Would you believe that the womenfolk personally nick-named every animal, all 6,844 of them? Names like Pebbles, Snooks, Polly, Bam-Bam, FeFe, Deitz-o-bo-hobo, Chee'chee, Dusty, Squirty, Sour-Blinky, Me'me, Stinky-Poo-Poo, Mad'eye, Toto, Poodie, Bubble'nose, Piepee, Stomper, Tubal, Baby, Muttzy, Txata, Wimpy, Whistle'britches, Peewee, TwoToToo, Waggs, Peanut, Stowaway, Notail, Booo, Soupy, Wiskers, Smirky, Moxxtaleo, You'vebeenduped, and thousands of more names. (You might think of a few names while you are reading.) I'm sorry this reads like a pet genealogy. I don't know how the girls came up with all these names, let alone remember which animal with its pet name. Besides, it's not like we have someplace better to go. We must sail on in God's purpose and grand plan.

All three of my boys had musical instruments; Seth and Japheth played the flute and other stringed instruments. The animals, especially the birds, enjoyed the music played on the flutes. Shem, Ham, and Japheth were also good at singing "a cappella." Oh my, the girls could shake the rafters singing "a cappella," and even the songbirds would chirp along. We spent our time with music, singing, working, and working some more. We also had a lot of fun as a family and with the animals, too. Hard work made our meals taste like a picnic every day. Then there was always that "Hide and Seek Game." Even some of the animals played it with the girls. However, these animals had an advantage: they had ears and a nose for the game. The dogs loved this game the most; the cats couldn't care less. I'm still wondering who came up with this game. I'm sure in the new world after this awful flood, it will be rediscovered, only to be given a complicated title. But I'm sure the children will simplify its name back to "Hide-and-Seek." This game belongs to two worlds and maybe even three.

God told Noah,

"Go into the ark,

you and all your household"

(Gen. 7:1).

Luther notes,

"There was that unbelievable wrath;

and the human mind

could not comprehend

that by the Flood

God would destroy

the entire human race,

all but eight souls.

~ Martin Luther
(who started the protestant reformation)

It's Still A Wonderful Adventure

It's now been over 142 days, and we have been sailing as the wind blows. At times, the ship remains still in the water. But when the wind blows hard, we sail very fast, and then we hear and feel a loud thump on the underside of the ship. We think it might be some large debris or perhaps a gigantic animal carcass floating dead in the water. Nevertheless, it isn't like we can pull the ark over and get out to see what we just ran over. For now, we are stuck in God's perfect will for our lives. This is why we enjoy each other, our work, and the opportunity to obey God. After all, as Kezia says, "It is a wonderful adventure."

Then it happened. After 150 days, the waters began to recede, and our ship was trapped on something huge, perhaps the tip of a great landmass. We are now loosely anchored in a safe place; the floodwaters have been receding for 150 days. This is where we will be stuck until the flood-waters have completely receded from the Earth. With each passing day, we could feel the ark settling down on solid ground. However, we remain sealed in the ark for our safety and that of the animals. Here we will be for many long days; we must have patience.

The girls started missing some of their shiny things, such as jewelry. Everything small, shiny, and pretty was turning up missing. They looked everywhere, and these colorful things were nowhere to be found. The girls knew that the boys would never want these things. It was quickly becoming a mystery until Shem found them. You guessed it, a pair of our unclean crows had found a way out of their cage and were stealing these pretty things, making a very elaborate nest. The ladies were happy to get their stuff back, but the crows squawked a lot and were not happy at all. The girls kept scolding the male crow, telling him he was a bad boy. Everyone was shocked when the crows started mimicking the girls, saying over and over, "Ca-Caw-Bad boy, bad boy." These bird brains wouldn't shut up; they were just talking, not thinking. Sometimes people do the same thing. Kezia went on to teach these crows some other words and phrases. Such as, "Are we there yet?" and, "Nope, not there, not there!" So, every day these birds kept squawking repeatedly, "Are we there yet?" or, "Nope, not there, not there." This sure didn't make our trip go faster. There were times we wanted to ring two necks.

Barefoot On The Ark

Japheth was always in the habit of taking off his shoes. Our clothes and shoes were not primitive before this flood; we had the best. Japheth had a comfortable high-top pair of shoes. But by habit, he had taken them off near the big cat cages and set them too close to one of the cages. The big cats had a great time playing with and destroying his shoes. The rest of this "wonderful adventure," Japheth will go barefoot. You would think that a 100-year-old boy would be a little more responsible.

After 310 days, our journey has been completed, and we are still sealed shut in the ark. After 40 days, I opened the upper window I had previously made, sending forth an unclean raven and a clean dove, to see if the land was dry and inhabitable. But the precious Dove could find no resting place outside the ark and returned to my hand. She was very weary and tired and glad to be back home. But the unclean raven never returned. He was delighted with the dead rotting animal carcasses floating on top of the dirty flood waters outside the ark. At this time, I sent the raven's mate out to meet its lover. Of course, neither of them returned; they were content with the rotting flesh outside the ark. Seven days later, early one morning, I sent the dove again out of the ark to see if there was dry land. Later that evening, she returned with good news in her beak, a plucked-off, beautiful green olive tree leaf. Our whole family shouted and celebrated, and prepared a great meal with singing and dancing.

Even the animals got excited because they sensed something good was about to happen. Seven days later, I sent the dove out of the ark again, but she never returned. I'm sure she went back to the olive tree to make a home and to build her kingdom. At this time, I sent her charming bridegroom out to meet her.

UNANSWERED PRAYERS

God is not the God of unanswered prayers.

Dead gods of wood and stone cannot care.

Stories of false gods are not true.

But Jesus Christ will change and answer you.

Jesus is the way, the truth, and the life,

for he alone conquers all sin and strife.

Do not linger long in sin.

Death awaits you at the end.

Call on the true God in your darkest nights.

He alone answers prayers and makes things right.

- James L. Eakins

Dear Reader,

We All Rode Over on the Ark,

We Just Weren't Aware of the Trip.

~ James L. Eakins

Finally Dry Land

Knowing there was dry land, I began removing the ark's wooden top. Later, I will use the dry wood to build an altar to the Lord and offer burnt sacrifices to him. However, the massive door of the ark was still sealed shut. It is so huge that only God can open it.

Our time on the ark was a total of 371 days. It was eleven days after my 601st birthday. When God opened the door of the ark, it sounded like a trumpet blast or a glorious shout. Then, God said to me, "It's time to walk out of the ark into your new world. Bring forth every living thing I have kept safe through my wrath." So quickly, at God's command, we opened every animal cage door and loosed them to let them go. Just like they entered the ark in pairs, they left it in male and female pairs. It took several days for the ark to empty, and many of these animals put on a spectacular show of joy as they departed from the ark. Our ladies helped the little helpless creatures out of the ark, for they had become their pets. I still marvel at how God put such a dreadful fear of man in all the animals, just after their ark encounter.

My wife and I walked out of the ark holding hands,

just like Shem and his wife, Japheth and his wife, and Ham and his wife. We were together and safe. What an overwhelming feeling it was to have gone through so much.

Days later, I found a large flat foundational rock to build a wooden altar on, using wood from the ark covering. This wood was the first to dry and would burn easily. After long prayers of thanksgiving to God and prayers for forgiveness, our family offered burnt offerings to the Lord from every kind of clean animal. It was hard for us because each of these animals we were sacrificing had become our friends. We cried for hours as we worshiped God. Innocent, precious blood was everywhere on the massive flat rock, and the fire and smoke kept ascending to heaven. Shem, while standing on this gigantic flat rock, slipped in a pool of blood while holding tightly to a beautiful lamb for sacrifice. His fall caused him to hit his head, making him temporarily blind, but later his vision returned. He also walked with a limp for the rest of his life due to injuring his thigh in this fall. We truly were grateful for God's everlasting mercy, preservation, and the salvation of the Lord for this future world.

God Put A Rainbow In The Sky

As we gazed at the eastern sky, the sun set behind us in the west. Still wiping the tears from our eyes, we then saw it: a beautiful, breathtaking triple rainbow in the clouds.

Then God spoke to us. "Behold, I establish my covenant with you, and with your seed after you; and with every living creature that is with you, of the fowl, of the cattle, and of every beast of the earth with you; from all that go out of the ark, to every beast of the Earth. This is the token of the covenant which I make between me and you and every living creature that is with you, for perpetual generations; I do set my rainbow in the clouds, and it shall be a token of a covenant between me and the earth. And it shall come to pass, when I bring a cloud over the earth, that the rainbow shall be seen in the cloud; And I will remember my covenant, which is between me and you and every living creature of all flesh; and the waters shall no longer become a flood to destroy all flesh. The rainbow is an everlasting covenant to this new world."

For perpetual years to come, there will be storms

and bolts of lightning, and dark clouds filled with rain. But God has made us a promise to all creation that he will never again destroy the earth with a worldwide flood. You can't catch a rainbow or hold one in your hand, but you can behold one in your heart. The rainbow is one of God's beautiful masterpieces.

Our family lived and farmed on the valley floors surrounding Mount Ararat for many years. It appears that God created an abundance of insects, bugs, and worms for the land, which remained cursed. My father, Lamech, taught me how to plant a vineyard and make wine when I was a young man. **I've always had a weakness and craving for wine—you know, the finest kind of wine.**

Living in this valley, Emzara and I will have the privilege of getting to know many of our grandchildren. In the years to come, Shem, Ham, and Japheth will venture forth with the first fruits of their children to other lands and will bear many more children to repopulate the whole earth. It will be intriguing to see what becomes of this New World and whether it will be as advanced as our old world before the flood.

As I carefully observed my three sons, Shem, Ham, and Japheth, I am convinced that from Shem and his descendants will come the promised seed that will crush the head of the serpent. This last Adam will forever redeem the world, just as God promised to the first Adam and Eve while they were in the garden. **Blessed be the Lord God of Shem.**

From the lineage of Shem
came Abraham, Isaac, and Jacob,
who is also known as Israel.
Through God's providence,
He loved the world so much
that He gave us Jesus Christ,
our one true Savior.

~ James L. Eakins

Just as the rainbow

assures us that a flood

shall never destroy the world,

so too does Jesus

assure us that the floods

of human sin

shall never drown

the faithful kindness

of the Lord.

~ Charles H. Spurgeon

I Believe The Story of The Flood

"Men say, 'I don't believe in the story of the flood." Christ connected His own return to this world with that flood: "And as it was in the days of Noah, so shall it be also in the days of the Son of man. They did eat, they drank, they married wives, they were given in marriage, until the day that Noah entered into the ark, and the flood came, and destroyed them all." I believe the story of the flood just as much as I do the third chapter of John. I pity any man who is picking the old Book to pieces. The moment that we give up any one of these things, we touch the deity of the Son of God.

-By D.L. Moody
1837-1899

"In the beginning God
and I believe the rest."

~ By true believers everywhere

BE STILL!
(A meditation from Mark 4:39 and Psalm 46:10)

When the storm rages, and the thunder roars,
and everything around you is shaken.

When your heart hurts to the very core,
and it seems all peace has been taken.

BE STILL!

When the sounds of danger cannot be ignored,
and your life is tearfully filled.

When the pain is too great,
and you cannot take more,
God's grace is sufficient.

BE STILL!

When your heart trembles on a dark, stormy night,
it seems that tragedy is near.

God's love will remove all your fright,
so be of good cheer-

BE STILL!

So, look to Jesus, who is power and might,
And he will calm your fears.

For he will command during your storm, peace-

BE STILL!

- James L. Eakins

The ark was not Noah's invention;
if God had not revealed His thoughts to him,
he would have perished
along with his fellow creatures.

Similarly, God must reveal through His Spirit
His thoughts of mercy and grace toward us;
otherwise, in our blindness and ignorance,
we would be eternally lost.

~ Author Pink

AFTERWORD

The captivating story of creation opens up end-less possibilities. After reading this book, you realize it is rooted in a true story, sprinkled with charming elements of fiction and storytelling.

This book is the third and final part of my series, "Stories Before the Flood." The story of Noah and the flood is captivating and holds many hidden treasures.

I hope this book inspires you to discover more amazing stories in the Bible.

- James L. Eakins

If you would like to contact the author,
please write to:
James L. Eakins
1302 South 18th Avenue
Ozark, Missouri 65721

GENESIS | CHAPTER 5:1-32
King James Version

This is the book of the generations of Adam. In the day that God created man, in the likeness of God made he him;

2 Male and female created he them; and blessed them, and called their name Adam, in the day when they were created.

3 And Adam lived an hundred and thirty years, and begat a son in his own likeness, and after his image; and called his name Seth:

4 And the days of Adam after he had begotten Seth were eight hundred years: and he begat sons and daughters:

5 And all the days that Adam lived were nine hundred and thirty years: and he died.

6 And Seth lived an hundred and five years, and begat Enos:

7 And Seth lived after he begat Enos eight hundred and seven years, and begat sons and daughters:

8 And all the days of Seth were nine hundred and twelve years: and he died.

9 And Enos lived ninety years, and begat Cainan:

10 And Enos lived after he begat Cainan eight hundred and fifteen years, and begat sons and daughters:

11 And all the days of Enos were nine hundred and five years: and he died.

12 And Cainan lived seventy years and begat Mahalaleel:

13 And Cainan lived after he begat Mahalaleel eight hundred and forty years, and begat sons and daughters:

14 And all the days of Cainan were nine hundred and ten years: and he died.

15 And Mahalaleel lived sixty and five years, and begat Jared:

16 And Mahalaleel lived after he begat Jared eight hundred and thirty years, and begat sons and daughters:

17 And all the days of Mahalaleel were eight hundred ninety and five years: and he died.

18 And Jared lived an hundred sixty and two years, and he begat Enoch:

19 And Jared lived after he begat Enoch eight hundred years, and begat sons and daughters:

20 And all the days of Jared were nine hundred sixty and two years: and he died.

21 And Enoch lived sixty and five years, and begat Methuselah:

22 And Enoch walked with God after he begat Methuselah three hundred years, and begat sons and daughters:

23 And all the days of Enoch were three hundred sixty and five years:

24 And Enoch walked with God: and he was not, for God took him.

25 And Methuselah lived an hundred eighty and seven years, and begat Lamech.

26 And Methuselah lived after he begat Lamech seven hundred eighty and two years, and begat sons and daughters:

27 And all the days of Methuselah were nine hundred sixty and nine years: and he died.

28 And Lamech lived an hundred eighty and two years, and begat a son:

29 And he called his name Noah, saying, This same shall comfort us concerning our work and toil of our hands, because of the ground which the Lord hath cursed.

30 And Lamech lived after he begat Noah five hundred ninety and five years, and begat sons and daughters:

31 And all the days of Lamech were seven hundred seventy and seven years: and he died.

32 And Noah was five hundred years old: and Noah begat Shem, Ham, and Japheth.

GENESIS I CHAPTER 6:1-22
King James Version

And it came to pass, when men began to multiply on the face of the earth, and daughters were born unto them,

2 That the sons of God saw the daughters of men that they were fair; and they took them wives of all which they chose.

3 And the Lord said, My spirit shall not always strive with man, for that he also is flesh: yet his days shall be an hundred and twenty years.

4 There were giants in the earth in those days; and also after that, when the sons of God came in unto the daughters of men, and they bare children to them, the same became mighty men which were of old, men of renown.

5 And God saw that the wickedness of man was great in the earth, and that every imagination of the thoughts of his heart was only evil continually.

6 And it repented the Lord that he had made man on the earth, and it grieved him at his heart.

7 And the Lord said, I will destroy man whom I have created from the face of the earth; both man, and beast, and the creeping thing, and the fowls of the air; for it repenteth me that I have made them.

8 But Noah found grace in the eyes of the Lord.

9 These are the generations of Noah: Noah was a just man and perfect in his generations, and Noah walked with God.

10 And Noah begat three sons, Shem, Ham, and Japheth.

11 The earth also was corrupt before God, and the earth was filled with violence.

12 And God looked upon the earth, and, behold, it was corrupt; for all flesh had corrupted his way upon the earth.

13 And God said unto Noah, The end of all flesh is come before me; for the earth is filled with violence through them; and, behold, I will destroy them with the earth.

14 Make thee an ark of gopher wood; rooms shalt thou make in the ark, and shalt pitch it within and without with pitch.

15 And this is the fashion which thou shalt make it of: The length of the ark shall be three hundred cubits, the breadth of it fifty cubits, and the height of it thirty cubits.

16 A window shalt thou make to the ark, and in a cubit shalt thou finish it above; and the door of the ark shalt thou set in the side thereof; with lower, second, and third stories shalt thou make it.

17 And, behold, I, even I, do bring a flood of waters upon the earth, to destroy all flesh, wherein is the breath of life, from under heaven; and every thing that is in the earth shall die.

18 But with thee will I establish my covenant; and thou shalt come into the ark, thou, and thy sons, and thy wife, and thy sons' wives with thee.

19 And of every living thing of all flesh, two of every sort shalt thou bring into the ark, to keep them alive with thee; they shall be male and female.

20 Of fowls after their kind, and of cattle after their kind, of every creeping thing of the earth after his kind, two of every sort shall come unto thee, to keep them alive.

21 And take thou unto thee of all food that is eaten, and thou shalt gather it to thee; and it shall be for food for thee, and for them.

22 Thus did Noah; according to all that God commanded him, so did he.

GENESIS | CHAPTER 7:1-24
King James Version

And the Lord said unto Noah, Come thou and all thy house into the ark; for thee have I seen righteous before me in this generation.

2 Of every clean beast thou shalt take to thee by sevens, the male and his female: and of beasts that are not clean by two, the male and his female.

3 Of fowls also of the air by sevens, the male and the female; to keep seed alive upon the face of all the earth.

4 For yet seven days, and I will cause it to rain upon the earth forty days and forty nights; and every living substance that I have made will I destroy from off the face of the earth.

5 And Noah did according unto all that the Lord commanded him.

6 And Noah was six hundred years old when the flood of waters was upon the earth.

7 And Noah went in, and his sons, and his wife, and his sons' wives with him, into the ark, because of the waters of the flood.

8 Of clean beasts, and of beasts that are not clean, and of fowls, and of every thing that creepeth upon the earth,

9 There went in two and two unto Noah into the ark, the male and the female, as God had commanded Noah.

10 And it came to pass after seven days, that the waters of the flood were upon the earth.

11 In the six hundredth year of Noah's life, in the second month, the seventeenth day of the month, the same day were all the fountains of the great deep broken up, and the windows of heaven were opened.

12 And the rain was upon the earth forty days and forty nights.

13 In the selfsame day entered Noah, and Shem, and Ham, and Japheth, the sons of Noah, and Noah's wife, and the three wives of his sons with them, into the ark;

14 They, and every beast after his kind, and all the cattle after their kind, and every creeping thing that creepeth upon the earth after his kind, and every fowl after his kind, every bird of every sort.

15 And they went in unto Noah into the ark, two and two of all flesh, wherein is the breath of life.

16 And they that went in, went in male and female of all flesh, as God had commanded him: and the Lord shut him in.

17 And the flood was forty days upon the earth; and the waters increased, and bare up the ark, and it was lift up above the earth.

18 And the waters prevailed, and were increased greatly upon the earth; and the ark went upon the face of the waters.

19 And the waters prevailed exceedingly upon the earth; and all the high hills, that were under the whole heaven, were covered.

20 Fifteen cubits upward did the waters prevail; and the mountains were covered.

21 And all flesh died that moved upon the earth, both of fowl, and of cattle, and of beast, and of every creeping thing that creepeth upon the earth, and every man:

22 All in whose nostrils was the breath of life, of all that was in the dry land, died.

23 And every living substance was destroyed which was upon the face of the ground, both man, and cattle, and the creeping things, and the fowl of the heaven; and they were destroyed from the earth: and Noah only remained alive, and they that were with him in the ark.

24 And the waters prevailed upon the earth an hundred and fifty days.

GENESIS | CHAPTER 8:1-22
King James Version

And God remembered Noah, and every living thing, and all the cattle that was with him in the ark: and God made a wind to pass over the earth, and the waters assuaged;

2 The fountains also of the deep and the windows of heaven were stopped, and the rain from heaven was restrained;

3 And the waters returned from off the earth continually: and after the end of the hundred and fifty days the waters were abated.

4 And the ark rested in the seventh month, on the seventeenth day of the month, upon the mountains of Ararat.

5 And the waters decreased continually until the tenth month: in the tenth month, on the first day of the month, were the tops of the mountains seen.

6 And it came to pass at the end of forty days, that Noah opened the window of the ark which he had made:

7 And he sent forth a raven, which went forth to and fro, until the waters were dried up from off the earth.

8 Also he sent forth a dove from him, to see if the waters were abated from off the face of the ground;

9 But the dove found no rest for the sole of her foot, and she returned unto him into the ark, for the waters were on the face of the whole earth: then he put forth his hand, and took her, and pulled her in unto him into the ark.

10 And he stayed yet other seven days; and again he sent forth the dove out of the ark;

11 And the dove came in to him in the evening; and, lo, in her mouth was an olive leaf pluckt off: so Noah knew that the waters were abated from off the earth.

12 And he stayed yet other seven days; and sent forth the dove; which returned not again unto him any more.

13 And It came to pass in the six hundredth and first year, in the first month, the first day of the month, the waters were dried up from off the earth: and Noah removed the covering of the ark, and looked, and, behold, the face of the ground was dry.

14 And in the second month, on the seven and twentieth day of the month, was the earth dried.

15 And God spake unto Noah, saying,

16 Go forth of the ark, thou, and thy wife, and thy sons, and thy sons' wives with thee.

17 Bring forth with thee every living thing that is with thee, of all flesh, both of fowl, and of cattle, and of every creeping thing that creepeth upon the earth; that they may breed abundantly in the earth, and be fruitful, and multiply upon the earth.

18 And Noah went forth, and his sons, and his wife, and his sons' wives with him:

19 Every beast, every creeping thing, and every fowl, and whatsoever creepeth upon the earth, after their kinds, went forth out of the ark.

20 And Noah builded an altar unto the Lord; and took of every clean beast, and of every clean fowl, and offered burnt offerings on the altar.

21 And the Lord smelled a sweet savour; and the Lord said in his heart, I will not again curse the ground any more for man's sake; for the imagination of man's heart is evil from his youth; neither will I again smite any more every thing living, as I have done.

22 While the earth remaineth, seedtime and harvest, and cold and heat, and summer and winter, and day and night shall not cease.

GENESIS | CHAPTER 9:1-29
King James Version

And God blessed Noah and his sons, and said unto them, Be fruitful, and multiply, and replenish the earth.

2 And the fear of you and the dread of you shall be upon every beast of the earth, and upon every fowl of the air, upon all that moveth upon the earth, and upon all the fishes of the sea; into your hand are they delivered.

3 Every moving thing that liveth shall be meat for you; even as the green herb have I given you all things.

4 But flesh with the life thereof, which is the blood thereof, shall ye not eat.

5 And surely your blood of your lives will I require; at the hand of every beast will I require it, and at the hand of man; at the hand of every man's brother will I require the life of man.

6 Whoso sheddeth man's blood, by man shall his blood be shed: for in the image of God made he man.

7 And you, be ye fruitful, and multiply; bring forth abundantly in the earth, and multiply therein.

8 And God spake unto Noah, and to his sons with him, saying,

9 And I, behold, I establish my covenant with you, and with your seed after you;

10 And with every living creature that is with you, of the fowl, of the cattle, and of every beast of the earth with you; from all that go out of the ark, to every beast of the earth.

11 And I will establish my covenant with you, neither shall all flesh be cut off any more by the waters of a flood; neither shall there any more be a flood to destroy the earth.

12 And God said, This is the token of the covenant which I make between me and you and every living creature that is with you, for perpetual generations:

13 I do set my bow in the cloud, and it shall be for a token of a covenant between me and the earth.

14 And it shall come to pass, when I bring a cloud over the earth, that the bow shall be seen in the cloud:

15 And I will remember my covenant, which is between me and you and every living creature of all flesh; and the waters shall no more become a flood to destroy all flesh.

16 And the bow shall be in the cloud; and I will look upon it, that I may remember the everlasting covenant between God and every living creature of all flesh that is upon the earth.

17 And God said unto Noah, This is the token of the covenant, which I have established between me and all flesh that is upon the earth.

18 And the sons of Noah, that went forth of the ark, were Shem, and Ham, and Japheth: and Ham is the father of Canaan.

19 These are the three sons of Noah: and of them was the whole earth overspread.

20 And Noah began to be an husbandman, and he planted a vineyard:

21 And he drank of the wine, and was drunken; and he was uncovered within his tent.

22 And Ham, the father of Canaan, saw the nakedness of his father, and told his two brethren without.

23 And Shem and Japheth took a garment, and laid it upon both their shoulders, and went backward, and covered the nakedness of their father; and their faces were backward, and they saw not their father's nakedness.

24 And Noah awoke from his wine, and knew what his younger son had done unto him.

25 And he said, Cursed be Canaan; a servant of servants shall he be unto his brethren.

26 And he said, Blessed be the Lord God of Shem; and Canaan shall be his servant.

27 God shall enlarge Japheth, and he shall dwell in the tents of Shem; and Canaan shall be his servant.

28 And Noah lived after the flood three hundred and fifty years.

29 And all the days of Noah were nine hundred and fifty years: and he died.

GENESIS | CHAPTER 10:1-32
King James Version

Now these are the generations of the sons of Noah, Shem, Ham, and Japheth: and unto them were sons born after the flood.

2 The sons of Japheth; Gomer, and Magog, and Madai, and Javan, and Tubal, and Meshech, and Tiras.

3 And the sons of Gomer; Ashkenaz, and Riphath, and Togarmah.

4 And the sons of Javan; Elishah, and Tarshish, Kittim, and Dodanim.

5 By these were the isles of the Gentiles divided in their lands; every one after his tongue, after their families, in their nations.

6 And the sons of Ham; Cush, and Mizraim, and Phut, and Canaan.

7 And the sons of Cush; Seba, and Havilah, and Sabtah, and Raamah, and Sabtechah: and the sons of Raamah; Sheba, and Dedan.

8 And Cush begat Nimrod: he began to be a mighty one in the earth.

9 He was a mighty hunter before the Lord: wherefore it is said, Even as Nimrod the mighty hunter before the Lord.

10 And the beginning of his kingdom was Babel, and Erech, and Accad, and Calneh, in the land of Shinar.

11 Out of that land went forth Asshur, and builded Nineveh, and the city Rehoboth, and Calah,

12 And Resen between Nineveh and Calah: the same is a great city.

13 And Mizraim begat Ludim, and Anamim, and Lehabim, and Naphtuhim,

14 And Pathrusim, and Casluhim, (out of whom came Philistim,) and Caphtorim.

15 And Canaan begat Sidon his first born, and Heth,

16 And the Jebusite, and the Amorite, and the Girgasite,

17 And the Hivite, and the Arkite, and the Sinite,

18 And the Arvadite, and the Zemarite, and the Hamathite: and afterward were the families of the Canaanites spread abroad.

19 And the border of the Canaanites was from Sidon, as thou comest to Gerar, unto Gaza; as thou goest, unto Sodom, and Gomorrah, and Admah, and Zeboim, even unto Lasha.

20 These are the sons of Ham, after their families, after their tongues, in their countries, and in their nations.

21 Unto Shem also, the father of all the children of Eber, the brother of Japheth the elder, even to him were children born.

22 The children of Shem; Elam, and Asshur, and Arphaxad, and Lud, and Aram.

23 And the children of Aram; Uz, and Hul, and Gether, and Mash.

24 And Arphaxad begat Salah; and Salah begat Eber.

25 And unto Eber were born two sons: the name of one was Peleg; for in his days was the earth divided; and his brother's name was Joktan.

26 And Joktan begat Almodad, and Sheleph, and Hazarmaveth, and Jerah,

27 And Hadoram, and Uzal, and Diklah,

28 And Obal, and Abimael, and Sheba,

29 And Ophir, and Havilah, and Jobab: all these were the sons of Joktan.

30 And their dwelling was from Mesha, as thou goest unto Sephar a mount of the east.

31 These are the sons of Shem, after their families, after their tongues, in their lands, after their nations.

32 These are the families of the sons of Noah, after their generations, in their nations: and by these were the nations divided in the earth after the flood.

ISAIAH | CHAPTER 54:9
King James Version

9 For this is as the waters of Noah unto me: for as I have sworn that the waters of Noah should no more go over the earth; so have I sworn that I would not be wroth with thee, nor rebuke thee.

EZEKIEL | CHAPTER 14:14-20
King James Version

14 Though these three men, Noah, Daniel, and Job, were in it, they should deliver but their own souls by their righteousness, saith the Lord God.

15 If I cause noisome beasts to pass through the land, and they spoil it, so that it be desolate, that no man may pass through because of the beasts:

16 Though these three men were in it, as I live, saith the Lord God, they shall deliver neither sons nor daughters; they only shall be delivered, but the land shall be desolate.

17 Or if I bring a sword upon that land, and say, Sword, go through the land; so that I cut off man and beast from it:

18 Though these three men were in it, as I live, saith the Lord God, they shall deliver neither sons nor daughters, but they only shall be delivered themselves.

19 Or if I send a pestilence into that land, and pour out my fury upon it in blood, to cut off from it man and beast:

20 Though Noah, Daniel, and Job were in it, as I live, saith the Lord God, they shall deliver neither son nor daughter; they shall but deliver their own souls by their righteousness.

HEBREWS | CHAPTER 11:7
King James Version

7 By faith Noah, being warned of God of things not seen as yet, moved with fear, prepared an ark to the saving of his house; by the which he condemned the world, and became heir of the righteousness which is by faith.

the ark was a preparing, wherein few, that is, eight souls were saved by water.

1 PETER | CHAPTER 3:20
King James Version

20 Which sometime were disobedient, when once the longsuffering of God waited in the days of Noah, while the ark was a preparing, wherein few, that is, eight souls were saved by water.

2 PETER | CHAPTER 2:5
King James Version

5 And spared not the old world, but saved Noah the eighth person, a preacher of righteousness, bringing in the flood upon the world of the ungodly;

MATTHEW | CHAPTER 24:37-38
King James Version

37 But as the days of Noah were, so shall also the coming of the Son of man be.

38 For as in the days that were before the flood they were eating and drinking, marrying and giving in marriage, until the day that Noe entered into the ark,

LUKE | CHAPTER 17:26-27
King James Version

26 And as it was in the days of Noe, so shall it be also in the days of the Son of man.

27 They did eat, they drank, they married wives, they were given in marriage, until the day that Noah entered into the ark, and the flood came, and destroyed them all.

LUKE I CHAPTER 3:23-38
King James Version

23 And Jesus himself began to be about thirty years of age, being (as was supposed) the son of Joseph, which was the son of Heli,

24 Which was the son of Matthat, which was the son of Levi, which was the son of Melchi, which was the son of Janna, which was the son of Joseph,

25 Which was the son of Mattathias, which was the son of Amos, which was the son of Naum, which was the son of Esli, which was the son of Nagge,

26 Which was the son of Maath, which was the son of Mattathias, which was the son of Semei, which was the son of Joseph, which was the son of Juda,

27 Which was the son of Joanna, which was the son of Rhesa, which was the son of Zorobabel, which was the son of Salathiel, which was the son of Neri,

28 Which was the son of Melchi, which was the son of Addi, which was the son of Cosam, which was the son of Elmodam, which was the son of Er,

29 Which was the son of Jose, which was the son of Eliezer, which was the son of Jorim, which was the son of Matthat, which was the son of Levi,

30 Which was the son of Simeon, which was the son of Juda, which was the son of Joseph, which was the son of Jonan, which was the son of Eliakim,

31 Which was the son of Melea, which was the son of Menan, which was the son of Mattatha, which was the son of Nathan, which was the son of David,

32 Which was the son of Jesse, which was the son of Obed, which was the son of Booz, which was the son of Salmon, which was the son of Naasson,

33 Which was the son of Aminadab, which was the son of Aram, which was the son of Esrom, which was the son of Phares, which was the son of Juda,

34 Which was the son of Jacob, which was the son of Isaac, which was the son of Abraham, which was the son of Thara, which was the son of Nachor,

35 Which was the son of Saruch, which was the son of Ragau, which was the son of Phalec, which was the son of Heber, which was the son of Sala,

36 Which was the son of Cainan, which was the son of Arphaxad, which was the son of Sem, which was the son of Noe, which was the son of Lamech,

37 Which was the son of Mathusala, which was the son of Enoch, which was the son of Jared, which was the son of Maleleel, which was the son of Cainan,

38 Which was the son of Enos, which was the son of Seth, which was the son of Adam, which was the son of God.

SHEM TO ABRAHAM
GENESIS | CHAPTER 11:10-32
King James Version

10 These are the generations of Shem: Shem was an hundred years old, and begat Arphaxad two years after the flood:

11 And Shem lived after he begat Arphaxad five hundred years, and begat sons and daughters.

12 And Arphaxad lived five and thirty years, and begat Salah:

13 And Arphaxad lived after he begat Salah four hundred and three years, and begat sons and daughters.

14 And Salah lived thirty years, and begat Eber:

15 And Salah lived after he begat Eber four hundred and three years, and begat sons and daughters.

16 And Eber lived four and thirty years, and begat Peleg:

17 And Eber lived after he begat Peleg four hundred and thirty years, and begat sons and daughters.

18 And Peleg lived thirty years, and begat Reu:

19 And Peleg lived after he begat Reu two hundred and nine years, and begat sons and daughters.

20 And Reu lived two and thirty years, and begat Serug:

21 And Reu lived after he begat Serug two hundred and seven years, and begat sons and daughters.

22 And Serug lived thirty years, and begat Nahor:

23 And Serug lived after he begat Nahor two hundred years, and begat sons and daughters.

24 And Nahor lived nine and twenty years, and begat Terah:

25 And Nahor lived after he begat Terah an hundred and nineteen years, and begat sons and daughters.

26 And Terah lived seventy years, and begat Abram, Nahor, and Haran.

27 Now these are the generations of Terah: Terah begat Abram, Nahor, and Haran; and Haran begat Lot.

28 And Haran died before his father Terah in the land of his nativity, in Ur of the Chaldees.

29 And Abram and Nahor took them wives: the name of Abram's wife was Sarai; and the name of Nahor's wife, Milcah, the daughter of Haran, the father of Milcah, and the father of Iscah.

30 But Sarai was barren; she had no child.

31 And Terah took Abram his son, and Lot the son of Haran his son's son, and Sarai his daughter in law, his son Abram's wife; and they went forth with them from Ur of the Chaldees, to go into the land of Canaan; and they came unto Haran, and dwelt there.

32 And the days of Terah were two hundred and five years: and Terah died in Haran.

1 THESSALONIANS | CHAPTER 4:1-18
King James Version

Furthermore, then we beseech you, brethren, and exhort you by the Lord Jesus, that as ye have received of us how ye ought to walk and to please God, so ye would abound more and more.

2 For ye know what commandments we gave you by the Lord Jesus.

3 For this is the will of God, even your sanctification, that ye should abstain from fornication:

4 That every one of you should know how to possess his vessel in sanctification and honour;

5 Not in the lust of concupiscence, even as the Gentiles which know not God:

6 That no man go beyond and defraud his brother in any matter: because that the Lord is the avenger of all such, as we also have forewarned you and testified.

7 For God hath not called us unto uncleanness, but unto holiness.

8 He therefore that despiseth, despiseth not man, but God, who hath also given unto us his holy Spirit.

9 But as touching brotherly love ye need not that I write unto you: for ye yourselves are taught of God to love one another.

10 And indeed ye do it toward all the brethren which are in all Macedonia: but we beseech you, brethren, that ye increase more and more;

11 And that ye study to be quiet, and to do your own business, and to work with your own hands, as we commanded you;

12 That ye may walk honestly toward them that are without, and that ye may have lack of nothing.

13 But I would not have you to be ignorant, brethren, concerning them which are asleep, that ye sorrow not, even as others which have no hope.

14 For if we believe that Jesus died and rose again, even so them also which sleep in Jesus will God bring with him.

15 For this we say unto you by the word of the Lord, that we which are alive and remain unto the coming of the Lord shall not prevent them which are asleep.

16 For the Lord himself shall descend from heaven with a shout, with the voice of the archangel, and with the trump of God: and the dead in Christ shall rise first:

17 Then we which are alive and remain shall be caught up together with them in the clouds, to meet the Lord in the air: and so shall we ever be with the Lord.

18 Wherefore comfort one another with these words.

1 THESSALONIANS | CHAPTER 5:1-11
King James Version

But of the times and the seasons, brethren, ye have no need that I write unto you.

2 For yourselves know perfectly that the day of the Lord so cometh as a thief in the night.

3 For when they shall say, Peace and safety; then sudden destruction cometh upon them, as travail upon a woman with child; and they shall not escape.

4 But ye, brethren, are not in darkness, that that day should overtake you as a thief.

5 Ye are all the children of light, and the children of the day: we are not of the night, nor of darkness.

6 Therefore let us not sleep, as do others; but let us watch and be sober.

7 For they that sleep sleep in the night; and they that be drunken are drunken in the night.

8 But let us, who are of the day, be sober, putting on the breastplate of faith and love; and for an helmet, the hope of salvation.

9 For God hath not appointed us to wrath, but to obtain salvation by our Lord Jesus Christ,

10 Who died for us, that, whether we wake or sleep, we should live together with him.

11 Wherefore comfort yourselves together, and edify one another, even as also ye do.

2 THESSALONIANS | CHAPTER 1:1-12
King James Version

Paul, and Silvanus, and Timotheus, unto the church of the Thessalonians in God our Father and the Lord Jesus Christ:

2 Grace unto you, and peace, from God our Father and the Lord Jesus Christ.

3 We are bound to thank God always for you, brethren, as it is meet, because that your faith groweth exceedingly, and the charity of every one of you all toward each other aboundeth;

4 So that we ourselves glory in you in the churches of God for your patience and faith in all your persecutions and tribulations that ye endure:

5 Which is a manifest token of the righteous judgment of God, that ye may be counted worthy of the kingdom of God, for which ye also suffer:

6 Seeing it is a righteous thing with God to recompense tribulation to them that trouble you;

7 And to you who are troubled rest with us, when the Lord Jesus shall be revealed from heaven with his mighty angels,

8 In flaming fire taking vengeance on them that know not God, and that obey not the gospel of our Lord Jesus Christ:

9 Who shall be punished with everlasting destruction from the presence of the Lord, and from the glory of his power;

10 When he shall come to be glorified in his saints, and to be admired in all them that believe (because our testimony among you was believed) in that day.

11 Wherefore also we pray always for you, that our God would count you worthy of this calling, and fulfil all the good pleasure of his goodness, and the work of faith with power:

12 That the name of our Lord Jesus Christ may be glorified in you, and ye in him, according to the grace of our God and the Lord Jesus Christ.

2 THESSALONIANS I CHAPTER 2:1-17
King James Version

Now we beseech you, brethren, by the coming of our Lord Jesus Christ, and by our gathering together unto him,

2 That ye be not soon shaken in mind, or be troubled, neither by spirit, nor by word, nor by letter as from us, as that the day of Christ is at hand.

3 Let no man deceive you by any means: for that day shall not come, except there come a falling away first, and that man of sin be revealed, the son of perdition;

4 Who opposeth and exalteth himself above all that is called God, or that is worshipped; so that he as God sitteth in the temple of God, shewing himself that he is God.

5 Remember ye not, that, when I was yet with you, I told you these things?

6 And now ye know what withholdeth that he might be revealed in his time.

7 For the mystery of iniquity doth already work: only he who now letteth will let, until he be taken out of the way.

8 And then shall that Wicked be revealed, whom the Lord shall consume with the spirit of his mouth, and shall destroy with the brightness of his coming:

9 Even him, whose coming is after the working of Satan with all power and signs and lying wonders,

10 And with all deceivableness of unrighteousness in them that perish; because they received not the love of the truth, that they might be saved.

11 And for this cause God shall send them strong delusion, that they should believe a lie:

12 That they all might be damned who believed not the truth, but had pleasure in unrighteousness.

13 But we are bound to give thanks alway to God for you, brethren beloved of the Lord, because God hath from the beginning chosen you to salvation through sanctification of the Spirit and belief of the truth:

14 Whereunto he called you by our gospel, to the obtaining of the glory of our Lord Jesus Christ.

15 Therefore, brethren, stand fast, and hold the traditions which ye have been taught, whether by word, or our epistle.

16 Now our Lord Jesus Christ himself, and God, even our Father, which hath loved us, and hath given us everlasting consolation and good hope through grace,

17 Comfort your hearts, and stablish you in every good word and work.

Study Notes:

Study Notes:

Study Notes:

Study Notes:

Study Notes:

Study Notes:

Study Notes:

Study Notes:

Study Notes:

Study Notes:

Study Notes:

Study Notes:

Study Notes:

Study Notes:

Study Notes:

Study Notes:

Study Notes:

Study Notes:

Study Notes:

Study Notes: